KUO_MEI 渦 媄

SaSa's Encounter: Conversing with Someone

Joannana Mei

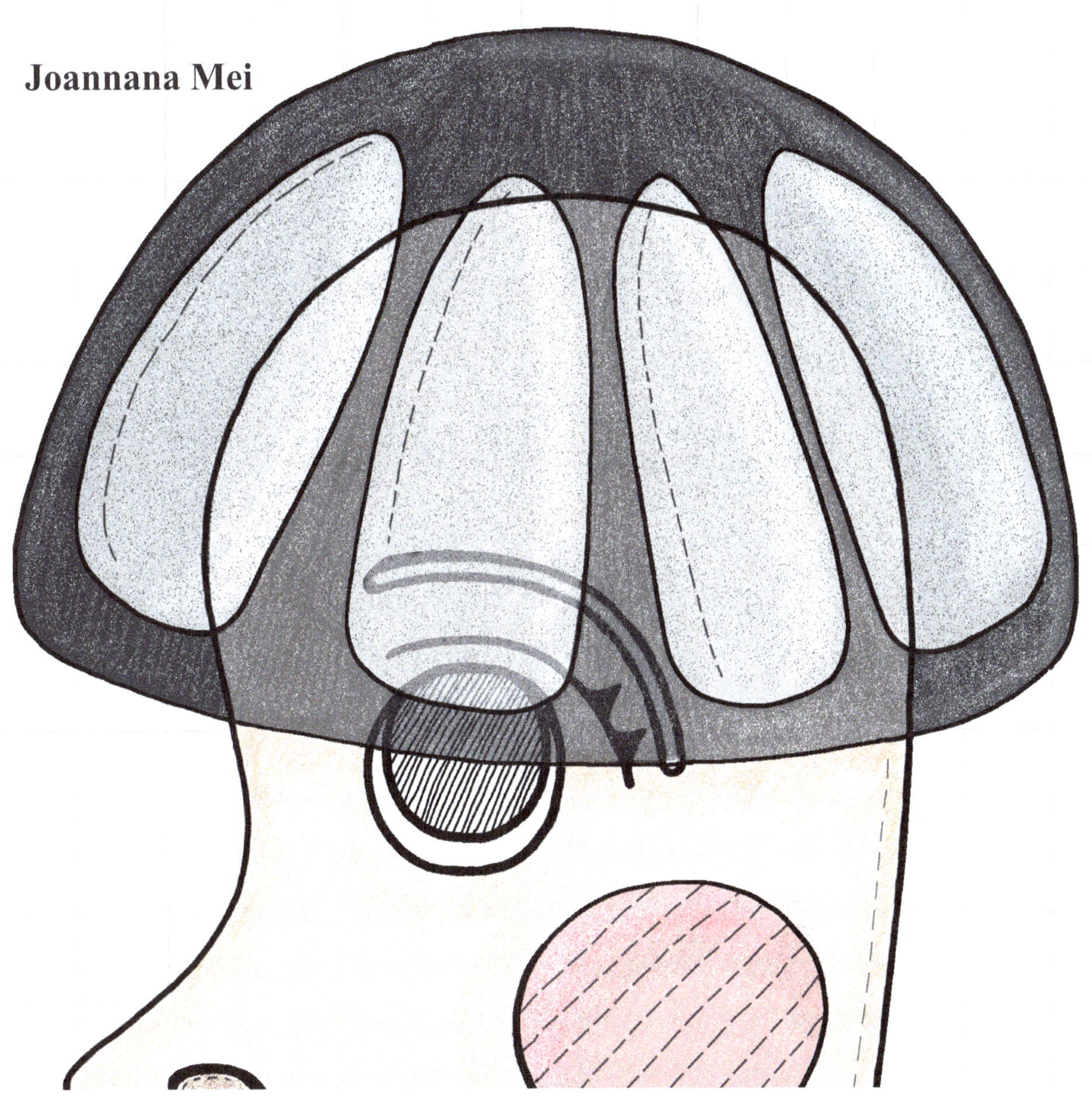

Looking back to the beginning, what was it for? Constant pursuit,
Constantly strengthening oneself, constantly exploring oneself,
Constantly enveloping oneself, do you still remember?
Some use knowledge as a shield, some use money as a pivot,
some use power as a foundation,
Some use beauty as a ritual, some use eloquence as a key, some use lies as a skill,
Countless pursuits, seeking the sugar coating of their respective needs,
Layer by layer wrapping outward, as if only thus could they find solace,
Could they gain a sense of security, could they draw closer to that vague desire,
Years of erosion and passing, tempering us,
wearing away many once-important things,
Already deeply buried,
As if able to temporarily forget many oscillating frequencies,
Believing that pain has nothing to do with oneself, as if, like an onion,
the changes in outer clothing conceal the inner originality,
Compared to the outer clothing, the originality within has become so small,
So small that it's almost invisible, lost night after night in darkness,
Forgetting the innate power that comes with us, how strong and beautiful it is,
Capable of instantly shattering the myriad layers of outer wrapping,
when all these coverings are shed,
Can we honestly face the naked truth,
discovering that what we seek lies in the beginning,
Finding the seed, and nurturing it into a thriving tree,
Feeling the clear spring gushing from within, able to penetrate all boundaries,
And lead us to the ultimate beautiful realm, which is also the ultimate goal.

Hello, I'm SaSa.
I've been hiding here for a long time. Did you find me?
Originally!
All the waiting was for this moment of encounter,
All the intertwining of chains existed for this moment.
I've been waiting, finally arrived,
I've been searching for a long, long time,
Now, I understand, this moment has finally come.

I don't know where I come from,
Who exactly am I?
I found myself somewhat different from you all.

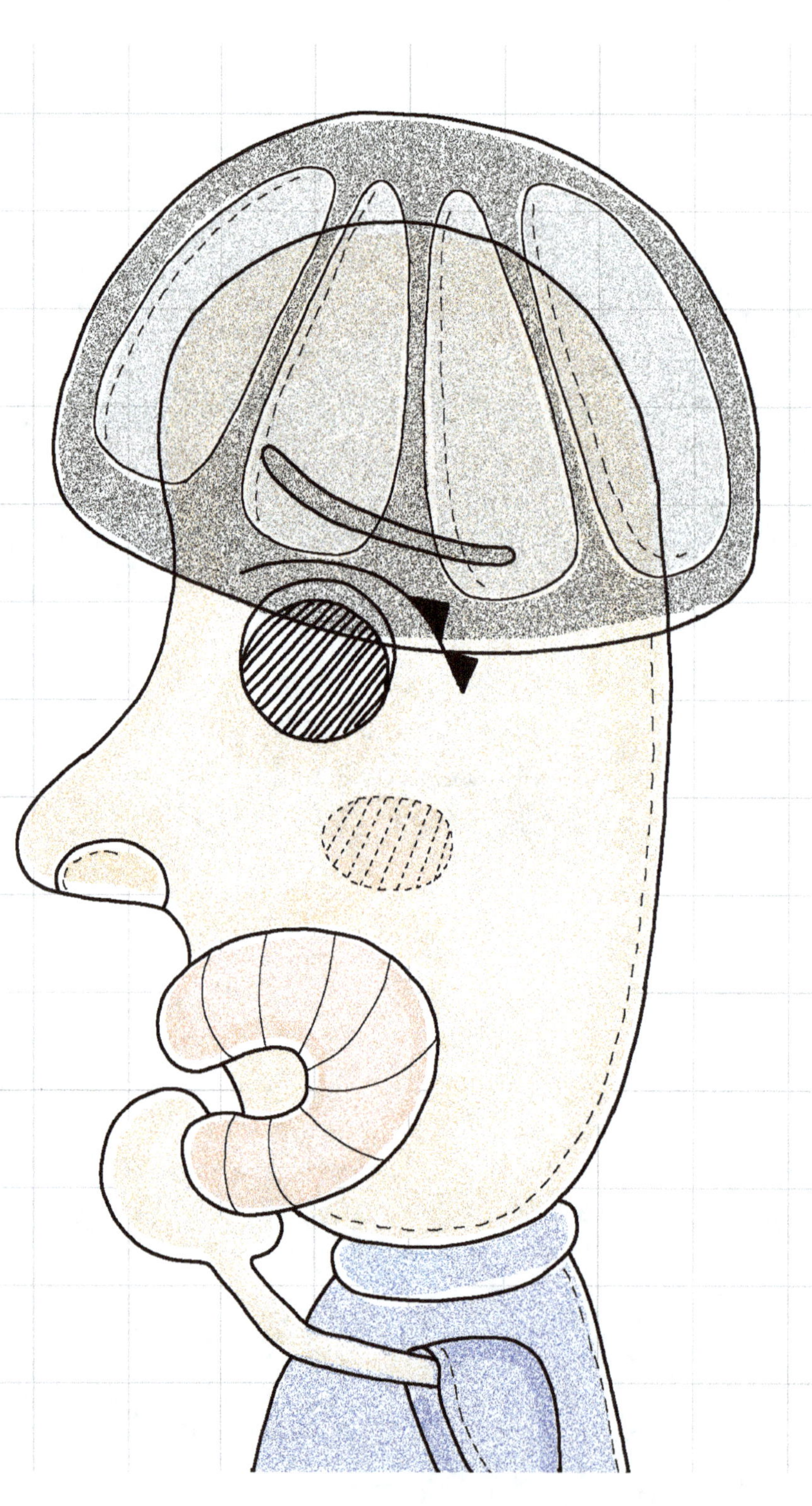

My head seems a bit long,
My nose is a bit big,
My lips are particularly thick.

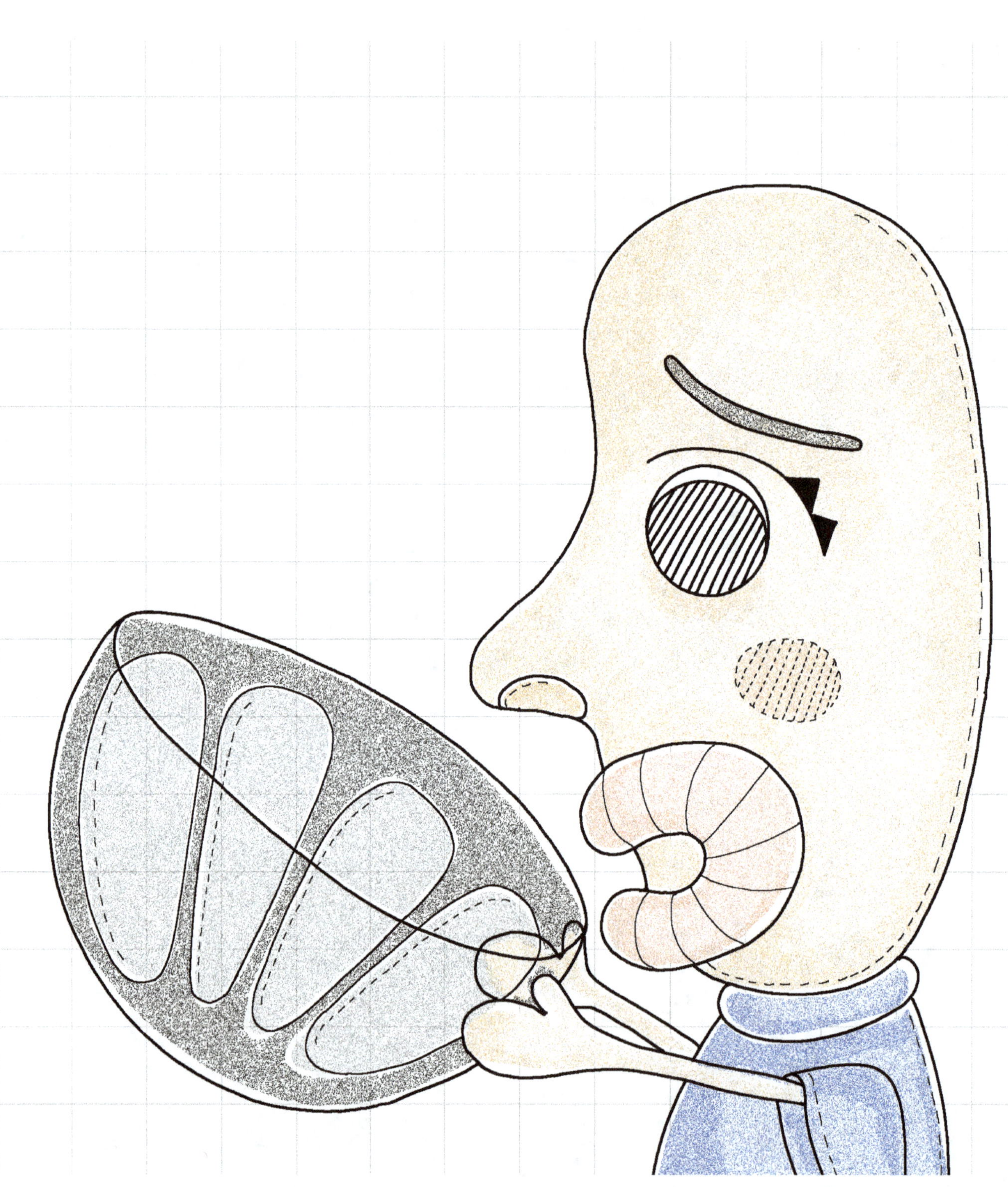

And, you see!
I can even take off my hair.
After removing it,
My bald head will be exposed.
You see,
It even reflects light! My heart is in turmoil.

I often feel a bit strange,
Unable to accept myself from the bottom of my heart.
Yes,
I always can't truly accept myself,
My heart is full of doubts and confusion.

Even the simple act of sitting down,
I can't do it easily,
Feeling difficult,
Every time it takes a lot of effort,
To sit properly,
To begin to appreciate the scenery after sitting down.
Often missing many beautiful sceneries.
I feel very sad,
Feel very lost.

This clear and transparent water,
This ripple of water is all my tears,
Traces of my fragility.
Beside the listless flowers,
Also become negative and dim because of my tears.

I don't know when it started,
I often look up at the sky,
Watching its unpredictable changes,
Immersed in the flow of daydreaming.
Thinking about those chaotic thoughts,
It could be described as painful,
It could also be described as curious about
the confusion of finding no answers.
Thinking why,
What exactly is it for?

But I never found the answer,
These questions are like endless darkness,
One by one they appear during the process,
After answering one, a new one emerges,
Continuously devouring me,
Shining in my eyes,
Making it hard for me to see what exactly is hidden in the darkness.

Just quietly observing like this,
Second by second,
Minute by minute,
Hour by hour,
Day by day,
Week by week,
Month by month,
Season by season,
Year by year,
Ten years, a hundred years, a thousand years, ten thousand years,
Millions of years,
I don't know how many years have passed.

What remains unchanged is that I still maintain the belief
and persistence of seeking answers,
What remains unchanged is my pain and confusion,
What remains unchanged is that I still look at things from the side,
Although experiencing a long time,
Still haven't gathered enough courage,
To face all these opposing sides squarely.

Looking at the sky,
Looking at the far behind it,
The ever-changing scenery in the sky,
Similar and dissimilar,
I gradually forgot myself.

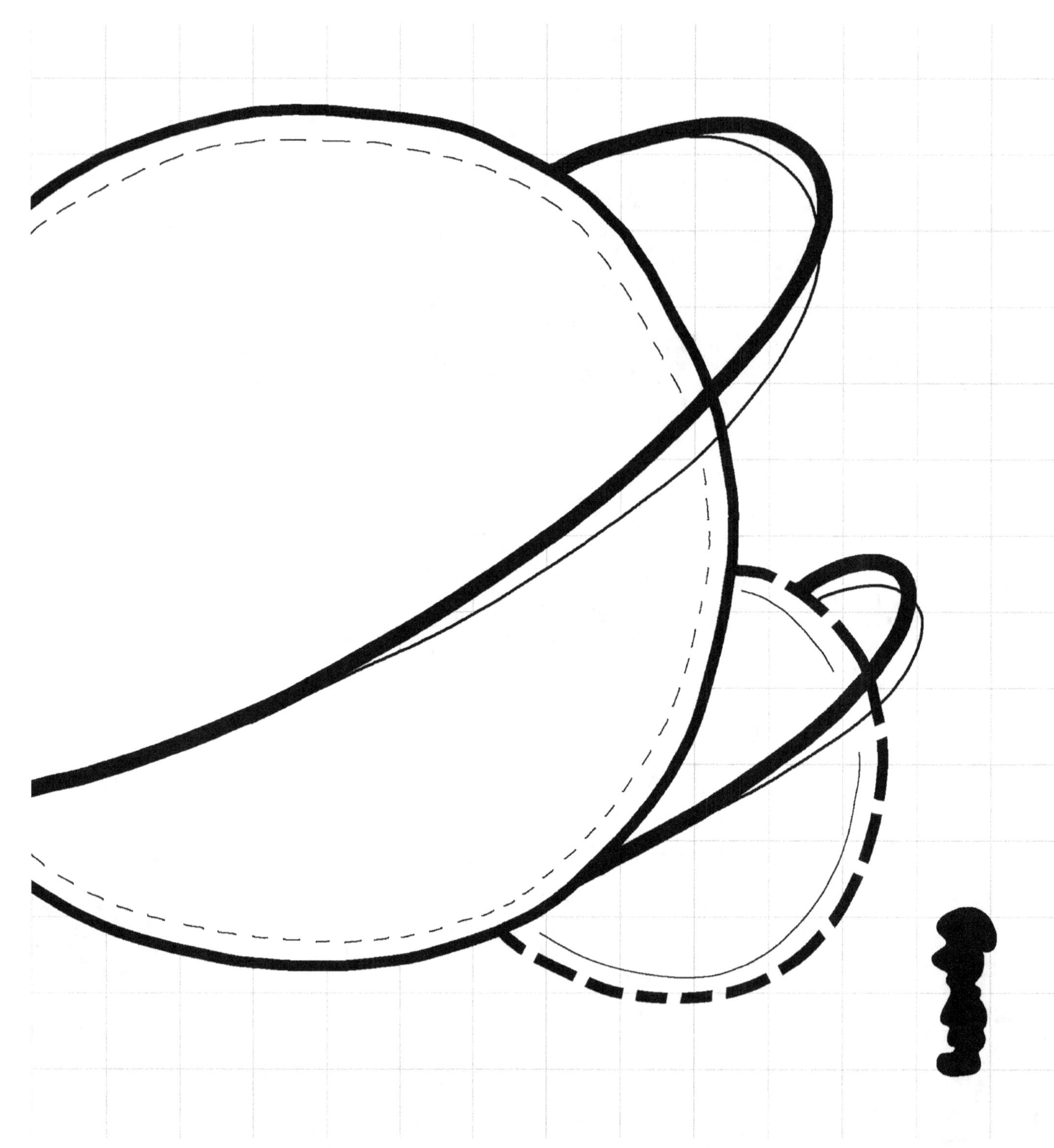

Continuously forgetting myself
Forgetting my own existence
Becoming small and insignificant.

Continuously becoming smaller,
So small that it's almost invisible,
Contracted to a point beyond zero,
Still continuing,
Following its natural laws,
Performing actions,
Going where it should go,
Seemingly scattered everywhere,
Yet seems united and cohesive,
So natural,
So free,
So charming.

Until the end,
Disappeared.
After I disappeared,
I understood,
This me is not that me,
The answer I've been searching for for thousands of years.
The answer appeared in an instant,
Springing up in a heartless space,
Beautiful scenes,
Unable to be described in words,
Unable to understand such existence,
Yet it's like merging hearts,
Such clear understanding.

Here,
From here continuously,
Warmly gushing out,
I discovered the wonderful connection
between myself and this world.

I started to love my nose,
My mouth,
Gradually accepting these unique features.

Also fell in love with this ever-changing hair,
And that long head.

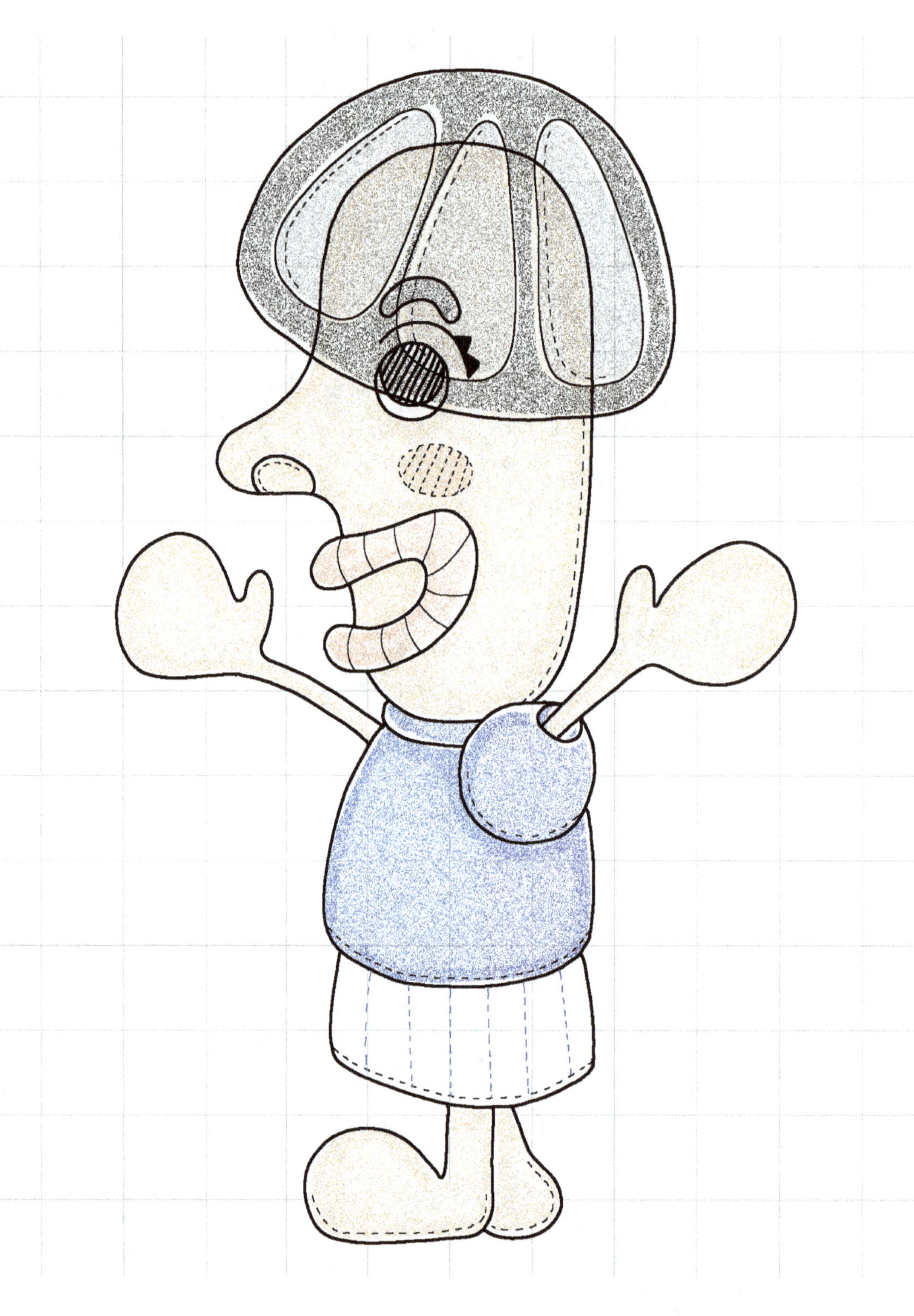

No longer feeling out of place,
Following the pace of nature,
I love myself more and more.

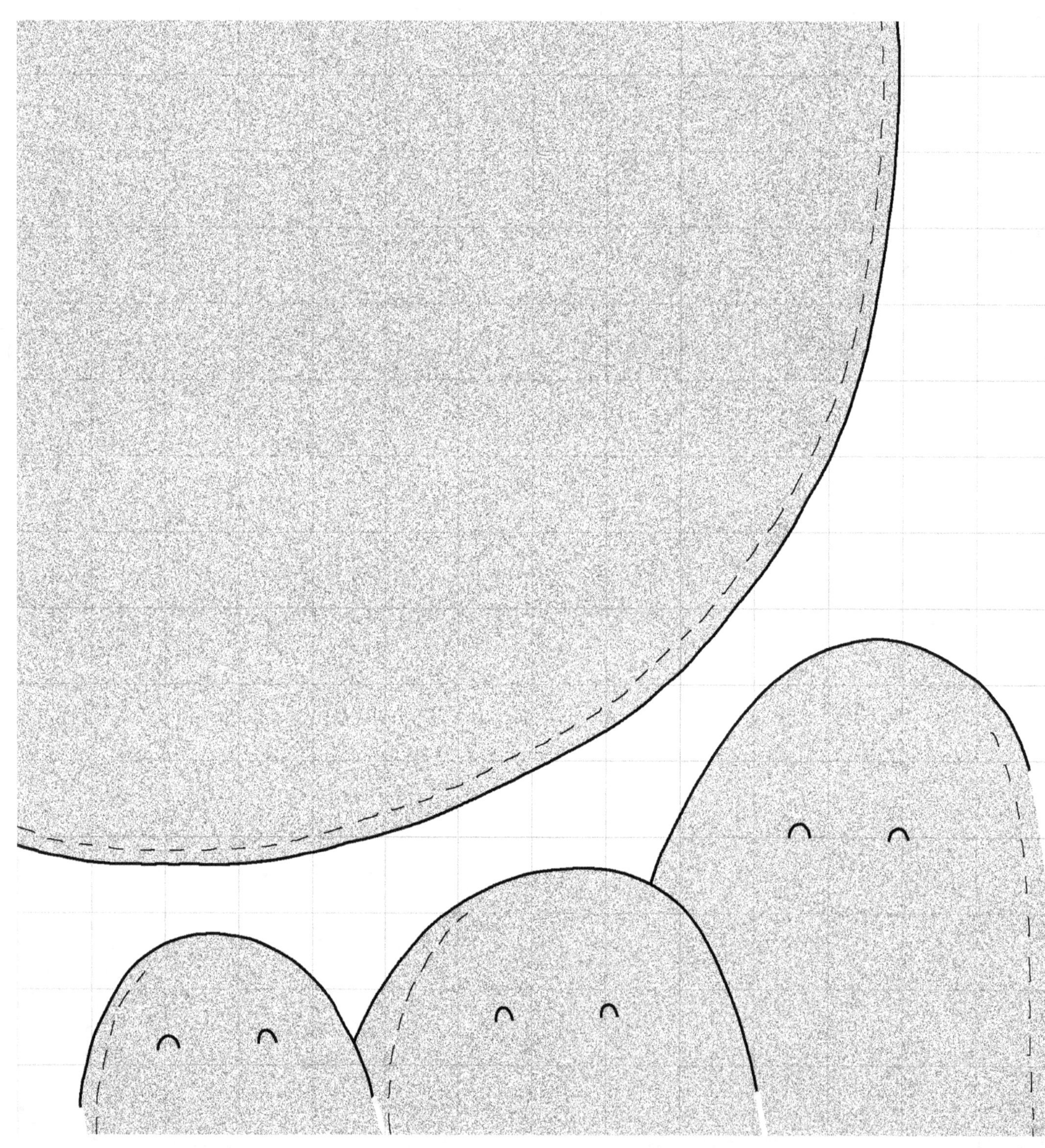

It should be said,
I love every single thing on earth,
All of it,
Expanding beyond the universe,
Including those I have never seen,
Never heard,
Never felt.

I met precious companions,
Exploring the mysteries of life together,
Sanil.

Daring to face everyone with positivity,
No longer doubting myself,
Believing energy spreads across every corner of the soul,
Filling every tiny corner,
Illuminating the darkness in the heart.

Hello,
I am SaSa with a lovely companion.
You found me,
I found myself,
Did you find your self in me?

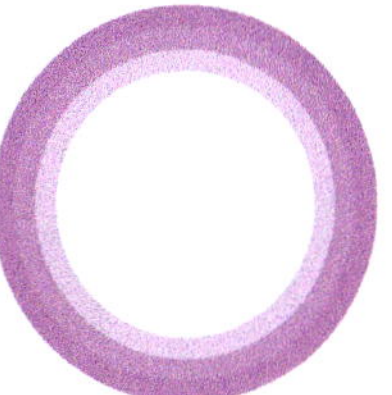

薩薩的邂逅：與某人交談

Joannana Mei

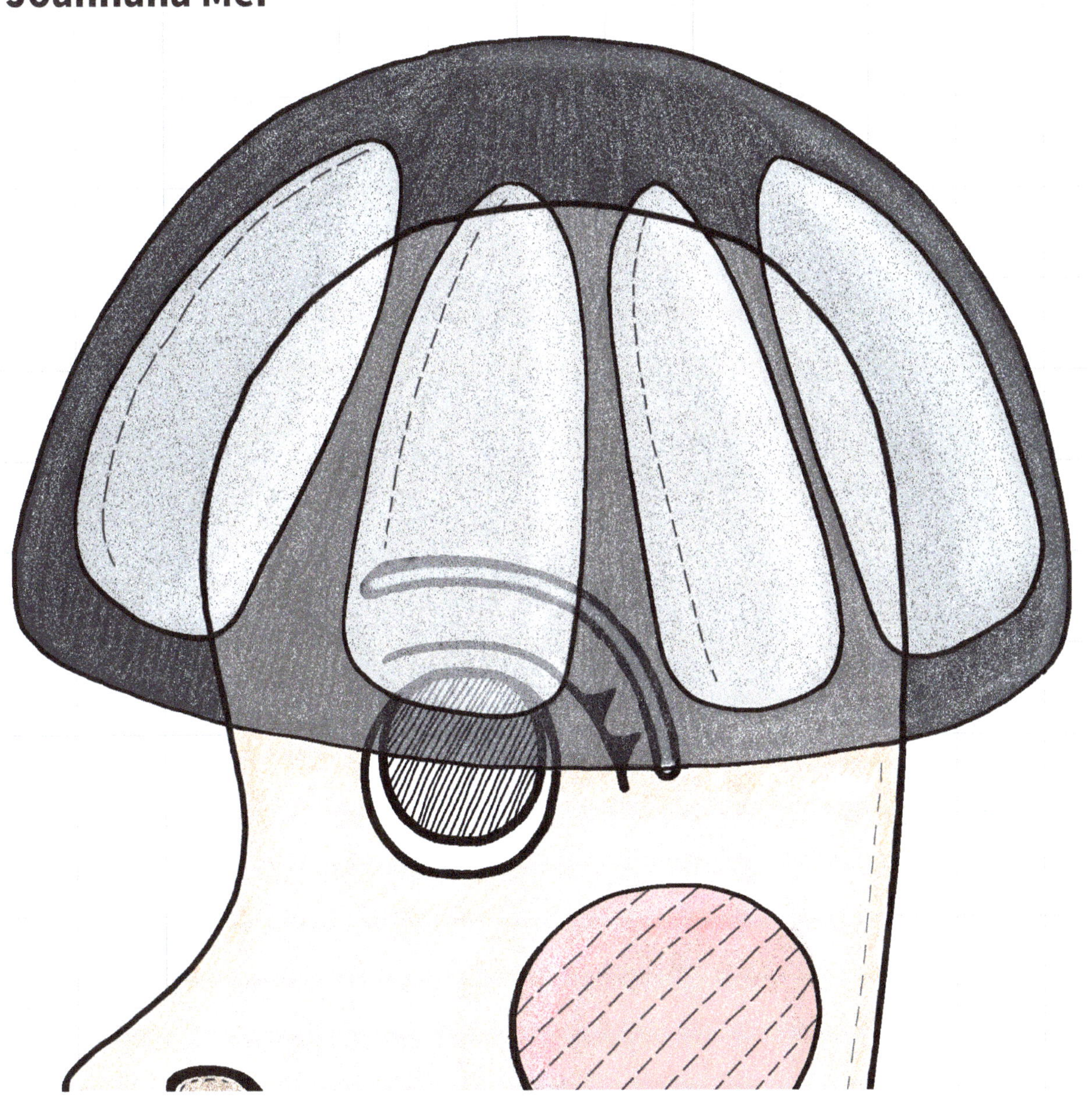

回溯之初是為了什麼？而不斷的追尋，
不斷的壯大自己，不斷探索自我，
不斷包裹自己，是否還記得呢？
有的以知識為盾，有的以金錢為樞，有的以權力為基，
有的以美貌為儀，有的以口才為鑰，有的以謊言為術，
無數的追求，尋找各自需求的糖衣，
一層一層的往外包裹，好像如此才能找到歸依，
才能獲得安全感，才更接近那模糊不清的渴望，
歲月的沖刷和流逝，磨礪著我們，磨去了許多曾經重要的事物，
已經被深深的藏起，
好像就能暫時忘卻許多震盪的頻率，
認為痛苦已與己不相干，彷彿洋蔥般，外衣的變化掩蓋了內心的原始，
裡面的原始之初相對於外衣，已經變得好小好小，
甚至看不見，夜夜迷失於黑暗裡，
遺忘了那與身俱來力量，是多麼的強大美好，
可以瞬間破碎那千萬層包裹的外衣，當褪去這些所有的包裝，
是否能坦誠面對那赤裸的本真，發掘所求之物便在於初始，
找到種子，並灌溉種子成茁壯的大樹，
所感受到的那股從內湧現的清澈源泉，可以穿透萬般的界限，
並將我們帶往最終的美麗境地，也是最終所求。

你好，我是薩薩。
我藏在這裡好久了，是你找到我的嗎？
原來呀！
所有的等待都是為了這一刻的相遇，
所有的鏈的交織，就是為了這一刻而存在。
我等到了，終於到達了，
我找了許久，找了好久好久，
現在，我明白了，這一刻終於來臨了。

我不知道我來自哪裡，
究竟是誰？
我發現自己與你們有些不同。

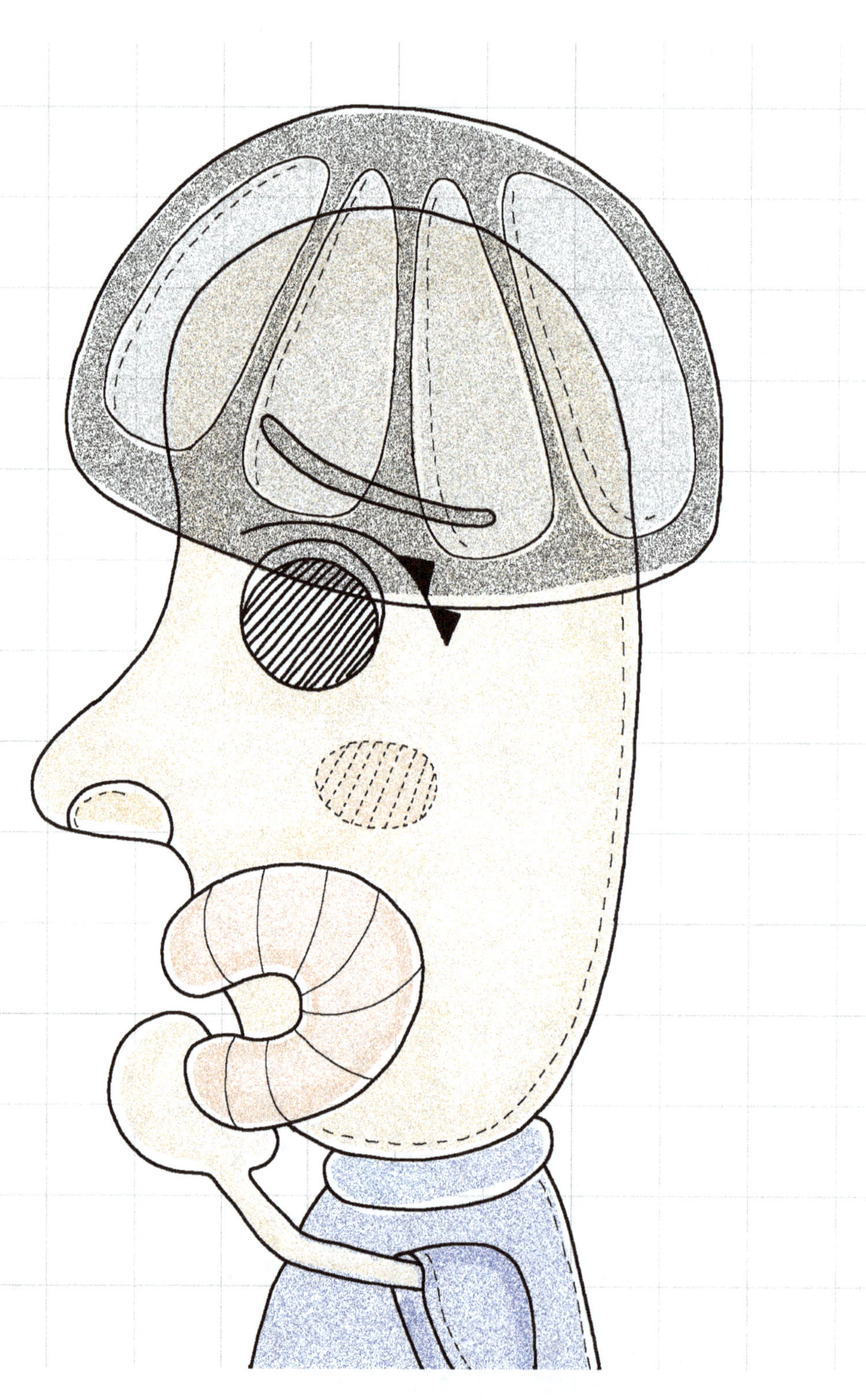

我的頭顯得有些長，
鼻子又有些大，
嘴唇也特別厚。

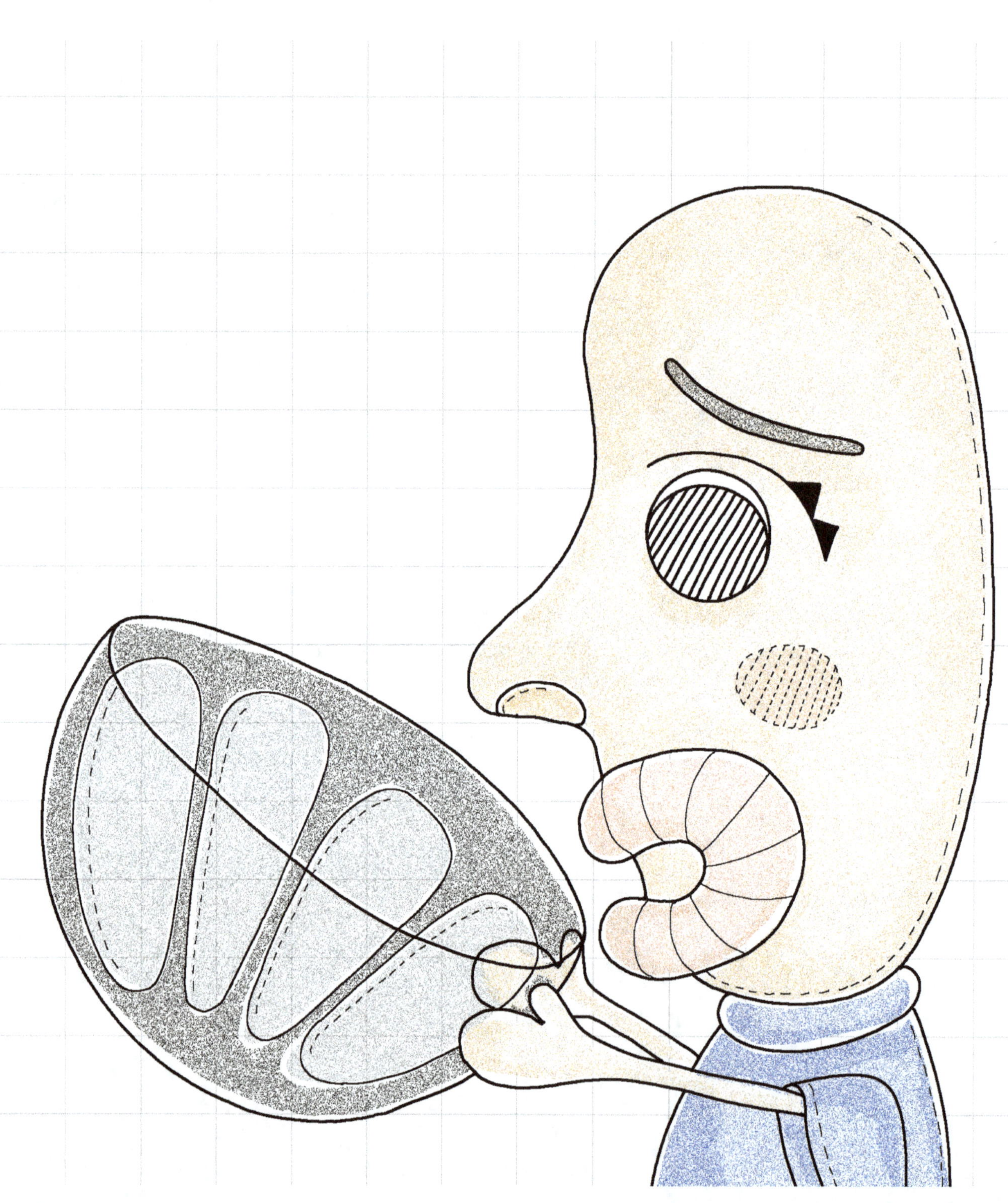

而且，你看！
我還能將我的頭髮拿下來。
取開後，
會露出我光溜溜的頭頂。
你看，
還會反光呢！
我的內心五味雜陳。

我經常覺得自己有些怪怪的，
無法發自內心的接受自己。
是的，
我總是不能夠實實在在的認同自己，
內心充滿疑惑與困惑。

甚至連坐下這個容易的動作，
我都無法輕易做到，
感到困難，
每次都要耗費很大的勁，
才能順利的坐好，
才能開始欣賞坐下之後的風景。
常常錯過許多美好的風景。
我感到很傷心，
感到很失落。

這清澈見底的水，
這一漥的水都是我留下的淚水，
是我脆弱的痕跡。
旁邊無精打采的花，
也因為我的淚水灌溉而變得消極黯淡。

不知從何時開始，
我經常的抬頭看著天空，
看著它的變幻難測，
沉浸在發呆的時間流裡。
想著那些雜亂無章的思緒，
可以說是痛苦，
也可以形容為好奇那些尋不到答案的困惑。
想著為什麼，
究竟是為什麼呢？

但始終沒有找到答案，
這些問題就像無窮無盡的黑，
在過程中——顯現，
解答完一個接著就會出現下一個的新星，
不斷的吞噬著我，
閃耀著我的眼睛，
使我看不清黑裡究竟隱含著什麼。

就這樣靜靜地觀察，
一秒一秒，
一分一分，
一時一時，
一日一日，
一周一周，
一月一月，
一季一季，
一年一年，
十年百年千年萬年，
千萬年，
不知究竟過了多少的年單位。

不變的是我依然保持著尋找答案的信念與執著，
不變的是我的那份痛苦和疑惑，
不變的是我依然的以側視人，
雖然經歷了漫長的時光，
始終沒有攢滿足夠的勇氣，
正視這些所有所有的對立面。

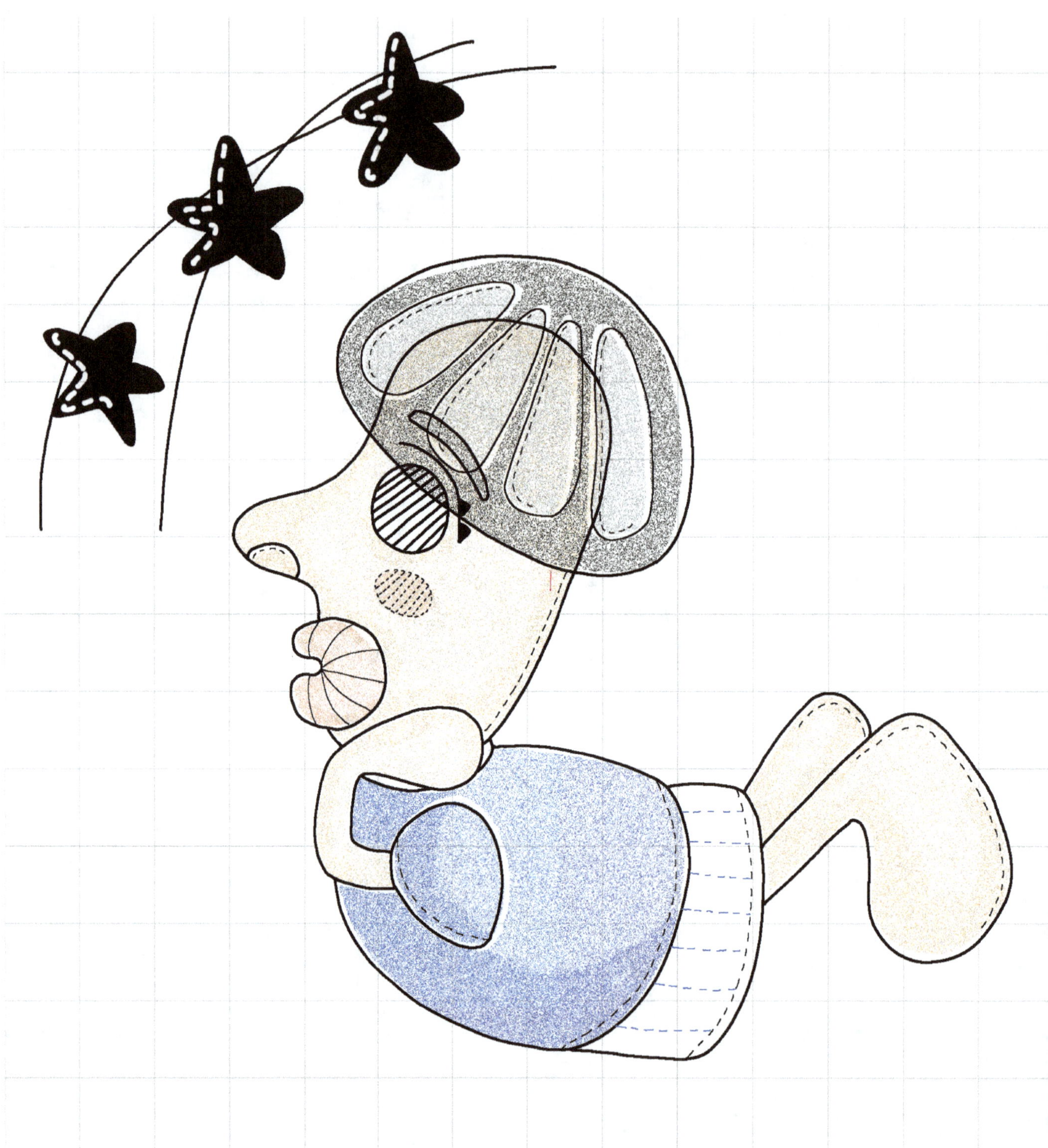

看著天空，
望向它身後的遠方，
天上不斷更迭的景色，
相似的與不相似的，
我漸漸忘了我。

持續的忘了我
忘卻了本身的存在
變的細小甚微。

不斷的變小，
好小好小，
小到幾乎要看不見，
緊縮到一個零界點之外，
還在持續的，
跟著它自然的法則，
運行動作，
去往該去的，
看似四處奔散，
又似團結凝聚，
這麼的自然，
這麼的自由，
這麼的迷人。

直到最後，
不見了。
在我不見後，
我明白了，
此我非彼我，
幾千年來尋找的答案。
瞬間答案，
蹦現在無心的空間，
美好的畫面，
無法用文字形容，
無法理解這樣的存在，
卻又像是心心相融，
那樣的透徹明白。

這裡，
從這裡不斷地，
不斷地暖暖的湧現出來，
我發現自己和這個世界有著奇妙的連接。

我開始愛上我的鼻子，
我的嘴巴，
漸漸地接受這獨特之處。

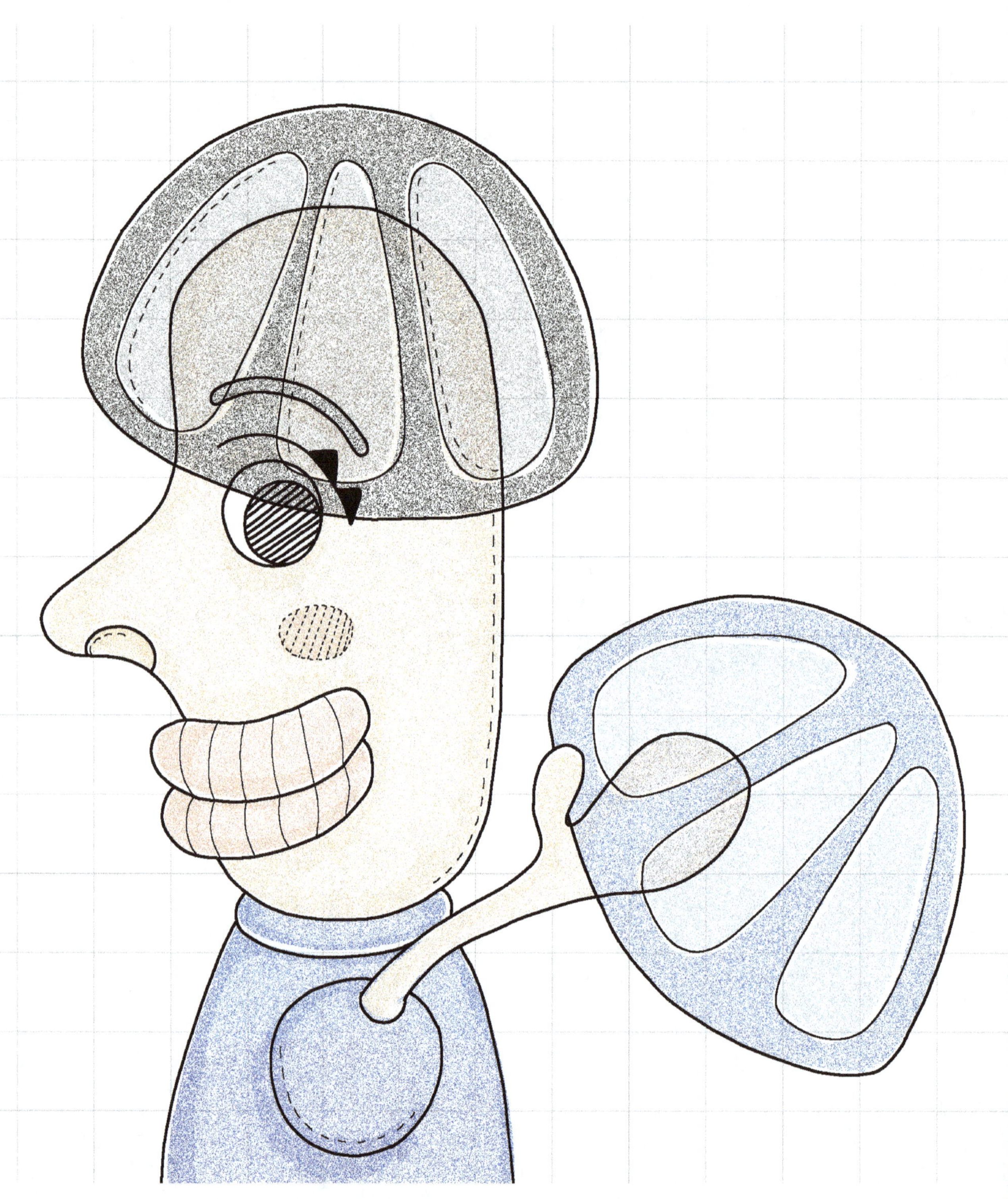

也愛上這變化無窮的頭髮，
以及那長長的頭顱。

不再感到格格不入，
順著自然的步伐，
我越來越愛自己。

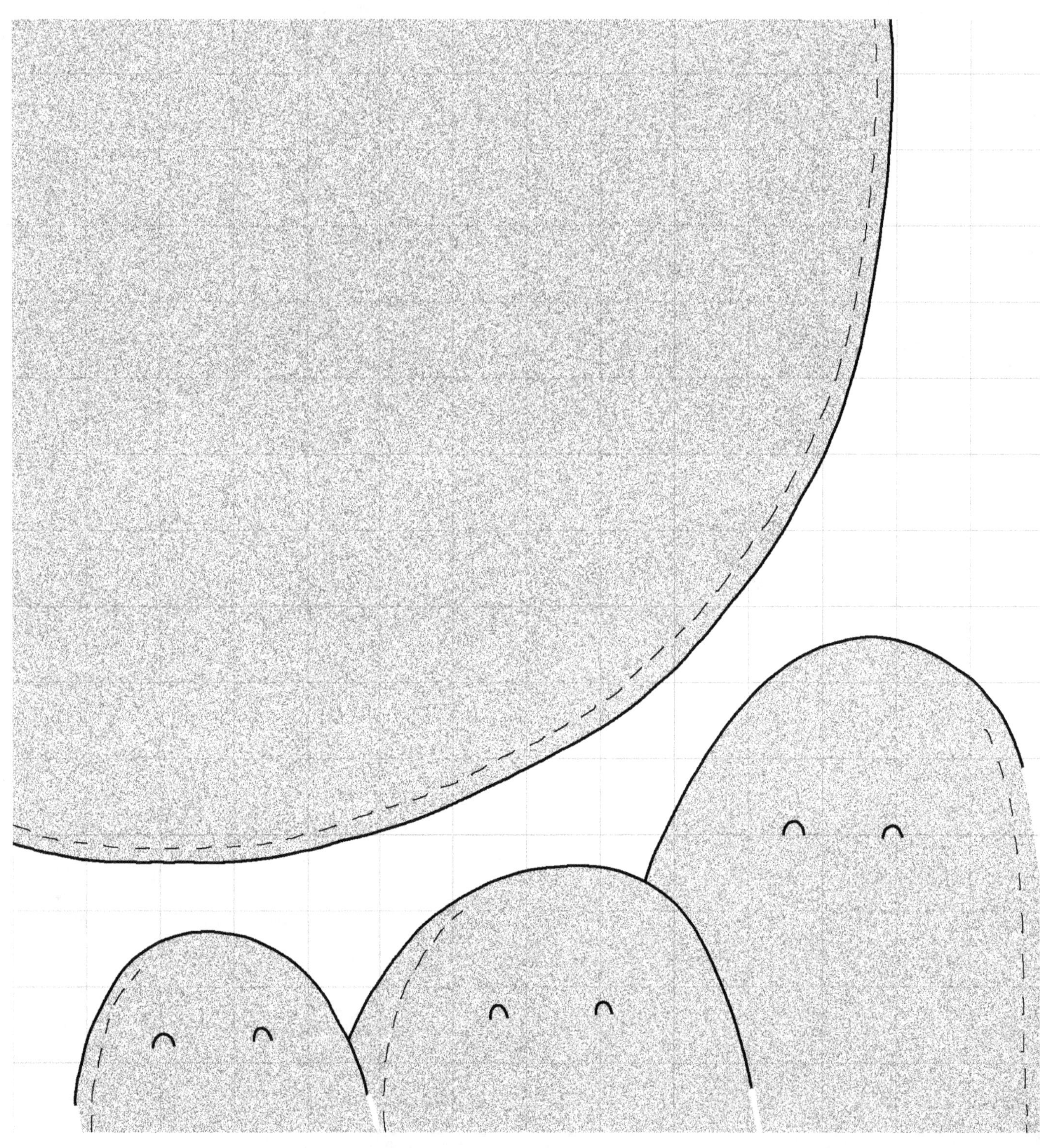

應該說，
我愛著每一樣地球的事物，
所有所有，
膨脹大至宇宙之外，
大致那些我未曾見，
未曾聽，
未曾覺到的一切一切。

我遇見了珍貴的夥伴，
與我共同探索著生命的奧秘旅伴，
薩尼爾。

敢於用正面去面對所有人，
不再懷疑自己，
相信的能量散遍心靈的每一處，
充盈著每一個細微的角落，
照耀心中的黑。

你好，
我是有著一隻可愛夥伴的薩薩。
你找到了我，
我找到了自己，
你找到你的我了嗎？

Joannana Mei

2024

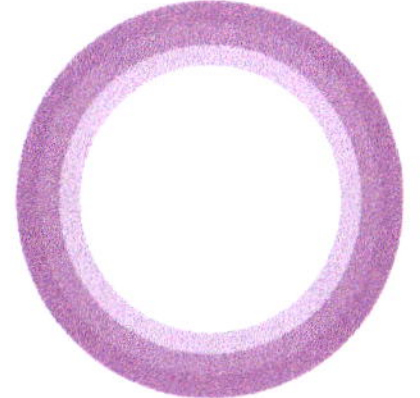